John Foster and Korky Paul

DRAGON POEMS

Oxford University Press

Oxford   New York   Toronto

For Tessa: K.P.

Oxford University Press, Great Clarendon Street, Oxford OX2 6DP
Oxford New York
Athens Auckland Bangkok Bogota Bombay
Buenos Aires Calcutta Cape Town Dar es Salaam
Delhi Florence Hong Kong Istanbul Karachi
Kuala Lumpur Madras Madrid Melbourne
Mexico City Nairobi Paris Singapore
Taipei Tokyo Toronto Warsaw
and associated companies in
Berlin Ibadan

Oxford is a trade mark of Oxford University Press

This selection and arrangement © John Foster 1991
Illustrations © Korky Paul 1991

First published 1991 Reprinted 1992
First published in paperback 1993

Reprinted 1994, 1995
First published in this hardback edition 1998

ISBN 0 19 276108 0 (paperback)
ISBN 0 19 276195 1 (composite)

A CIP catalogue record for this book is available from the British
Library

Set by FWT Studios, England

Printed in Hong Kong

Acknowledgements

The editor and publisher are grateful for permission to include the
following copyright material in this anthology.

Moira Andrew, 'Portrait of a Dragon', © by Moira Andrew.
Reprinted by permission of the author.

Tony Bradman, 'The Pet', © 1991 by Tony Bradman. Reprinted by
permission of the author.

Max Fatchen, 'Anyone Wanting a Fiery Dragon' from *A Paddock of
Poems* (Omnibus/Puffin, Adelaide 1987) © Max Fatchen 1987.
Reprinted by permission of John Johnson Ltd.

Eric Finney, 'Dragon Band' and 'The Ice Dragons', © 1991 by Eric
Finney. Reprinted by permission of the author.

John Foster, 'The School for Young Dragons', © 1991 by John
Foster.

David Harmer, 'Never Trust Dragons' © 1991 by David Harmer.
Reprinted by permission of the author.

Julie Holder, 'How Dragons Hide', 'The Lonely Dragon', 'Is There a
Dragon in the House?', © 1991 by Julie Holder.

X. J. Kennedy, 'My Dragon' from *The Phantom Ice-Cream Man*
(1979), © 1975, 1977, 1978, 1979 by X. J. Kennedy. Reprinted by
permission of Curtis Brown Ltd.

Ian Larmont, 'The Last Dragon', © 1991 by Ian Larmont. Reprinted
by permission of the author.

Daphne Lister 'The Dragon' from *Gingerbread Pigs & Other Rhymes*
(Transworld 1980). © by Daphne Lister. Reprinted by permission of
the author.

Lilian Moore, 'Lost and Found' from *See My Lovely Poison Ivy*, ©
1975 by Lilian Moore. Reprinted by permission of Marian Reiner for
the author.

Judith Nicholls, 'Dragonbirth', © 1991 by Judith Nicholls. Reprinted
by permission of the author.

Jack Prelutsky, 'Happy Birthday, Dear Dragon' from *The New Kid
On The Block,* © 1984 by Jack Prelutsky. Reprinted by permission of
William Heinemann Ltd., and Greenwillow Books, William Morrow
& Co. Inc.

Irene Rawnsley, 'Dragon's Breath' from *Dog's Dinner,* by Irene
Rawnsley. Reprinted by permission of Methuen Childrens Books.

William Jay Smith, 'The Toaster' from *Laughing Time,* © 1955,
1957, 1980, 1990 by William Jay Smith. Reprinted by permission of
Farrar Straus & Giroux Inc.

Charles Thomson, 'A Dragon in the Classroom', © 1991 Charles
Thomson. Reprinted by permission of the author.

Clive Webster, 'No Contest', 'Drawback', © 1991 by Clive Webster,
Reprinted by permission of the author.

Colin West, 'Jocelyn, My Dragon' from *The Best of West* (Hutchinson
1990) ©1990 by Colin West. Reprinted by permission of the author.

Raymond Wilson, 'The Grateful Dragon' © 1991 by Raymond
Wilson. Reprinted by permission of the author.

CONTENTS

4

Happy Birthday, Dear Dragon

There were rumbles of strange jubilation
in a dark, subterranean lair,
for the dragon was having a birthday,
and his colleagues were gathering there.
'HOORAH!' groaned the trolls and the ogres
as they pelted each other with stones.
'HOORAH!' shrieked a sphinx and a griffin,
and the skeletons rattled their bones.

'HOORAH!' screamed the queen of the demons.
'HOORAH!' boomed a giant. 'REJOICE!'
'Hoorah!' piped a tiny hobgoblin
in an almost inaudible voice.
'HOORAH!' cackled rapturous witches.
'Hoorahhhhhh!' hissed a basilisk too.
Then they howled in cacophonous chorus,
'HAPPY BIRTHDAY,
DEAR DRAGON,
TO YOU!'

They whistled, they squawked, they applauded,
as they gleefully brought forth the cake.
'OH, THANK YOU!'
he thundered with pleasure
in a bass that made every ear ache.
Then puffing his chest to the fullest,
and taking deliberate aim,
the dragon huffed once at the candles –

and
the candles
all burst
into
flame!

Jack Prelutsky

Portrait of a Dragon

If I were an artist
I'd paint the portrait
   of a dragon.

To do a proper job
I'd borrow colours
   from the world.

For his back I'd
need a mountain range,
   all misty-blue.

For spikes I'd use
dark fir trees pointing
   to the sky.

For overlapping scales
I'd squeeze dye from
   bright anemones.

I'd gild his claws
like shining swords
   with starlight.

His tail would be
a river, silver
   in the sun.

For his head, the
secret green of forests
   and deep seas.

And his eyes would
glow like embers in
   a tinker's fire.

But I'd keep the best
till last. For his
   hot breath

I'd use all reds and
yellows – crocus, saffron,
   peony, poppy,

geranium, cyclamen, rose –
and fierce orange flames
   from a marigold.

Moira Andrew

The Pet

My mum gave me some money
   To buy myself a treat;
She said I could buy anything
   (So long as it wasn't sweets).

So off I went to spend it.
   I wandered round the shops,
I couldn't find a thing to buy . . .
   Then something made me stop.

There in a pet shop window
   I saw a flash of fire;
I saw some scales and burning eyes
   And I knew my heart's desire.

I gave the man my money.
   He handed me a lead.
Then I walked out of the pet shop
   With the only pet I need.

A pet with wings and gleaming fangs,
   With skin that's shiny green;
With claws, and a tail that's longer
   Than any tail you've seen.

A pet whose breath is orange flame,
   Whose ears both hiss with steam,
Who'll fly me to the land of clouds
   And to the land of dreams.

But first I'd better go home.
   I hope that it's OK . . .
I hope my mum will like my pet.
   I wonder what she'll say?

Tony Bradman

No Contest

The little boy was in distress –
'Dad,' he yelled. 'Quick, help!
A fiery dragon's just got Mum,
She's fighting it herself.'

'Don't worry, son,' his dad replied,
Ignoring his son's pleading.
'The dragon's in with half a chance'–
And carried on his reading.

Clive Webster

My Dragon

I have a purple dragon
With a long brass tail that clangs,
And anyone not nice to me
Soon feels his fiery fangs,

So if you tell me I'm a dope
Or call my muscles jelly,
You just might dwell a billion years
Inside his boiling belly.

X. J. Kennedy

A Dragon in the Classroom

There's a dragon in the classroom:
its body is a box,
its head's a plastic waste-bin,
its eyes are broken clocks,

its legs are cardboard tubes,
its claws are toilet rolls,
its tongue's my dad's old tie
(that's why it's full of holes).

'Oh, what a lovely dragon,'
our teacher smiled and said.
'You *are* a pretty dragon,'
she laughed and stroked its head.

'Oh no, I'm not,' he snorted,
SNAP! SNAP! he moved his jaw
and chased our screaming teacher
along the corridor.

Charles Thomson

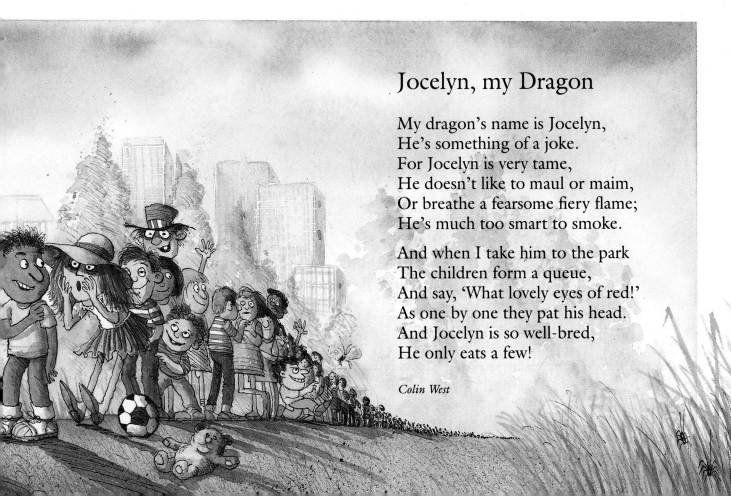

Jocelyn, my Dragon

My dragon's name is Jocelyn,
He's something of a joke.
For Jocelyn is very tame,
He doesn't like to maul or maim,
Or breathe a fearsome fiery flame;
He's much too smart to smoke.

And when I take him to the park
The children form a queue,
And say, 'What lovely eyes of red!'
As one by one they pat his head.
And Jocelyn is so well-bred,
He only eats a few!

Colin West

Dragonbirth

In the midnight mists
of long ago
on a far-off mountainside
there stood
a wild oak wood . . .

In the wild, wet wood
there grew an oak;
beneath the oak
there slept a cave
and in that cave
the mosses crept.
Beneath the moss
there lay a stone,
beneath the stone
there lay an egg,
and in that egg
there was a crack.
From that crack
there breathed a flame;
from that flame
there burst a fire,
and from that fire

dragon came.

Judith Nicholls

Dragon's Breath

One winter
when the world was still
a dragon came into the cold;
he rattled all the icicles
and shook his scales of gold.

He spread his body on the earth
to make the flowers grow;
he snorted
with his fiery breath
and melted all the snow.

He snorted
with his fiery breath
to set the river free;
he coiled his golden tail
around a budding hazel tree.

He coiled his golden tail
until catkins began to shake,
then spread his wings
and flew
to warm another world awake.

Irene Rawnsley

How Dragons Hide

Dragon babies
Are fat and pudgy
They slide down the helter-skelter
Of Mother Dragon's back
They swing on her tail
They pull faces at themselves
In the mirror of her scales.

Dragon babies
Bibble and babble
They blow smoke bubbles
They dribble small flames
They suck sun hot pebbles
And crunch them in sharp little teeth.

Dragon babies
Play with jingly jewels
They leave them where they fall
To become buried treasure
They throw them in the river
To see the splashes.

Dragon babies
Clap their small wings
Pretending they are old enough to fly
They roll in the river mud
To make small clouds of steam.
Their Mother lies like a low green hill
And watches over them.

If they hear the sounds of people
They hide in the long green grass
Still as stones they lie
Their Mother hides her head
And becomes a low green hill.

They hold their fiery breath
And the people pass
Seeing only stones in the grass
And a low green hill.

Julie Holder

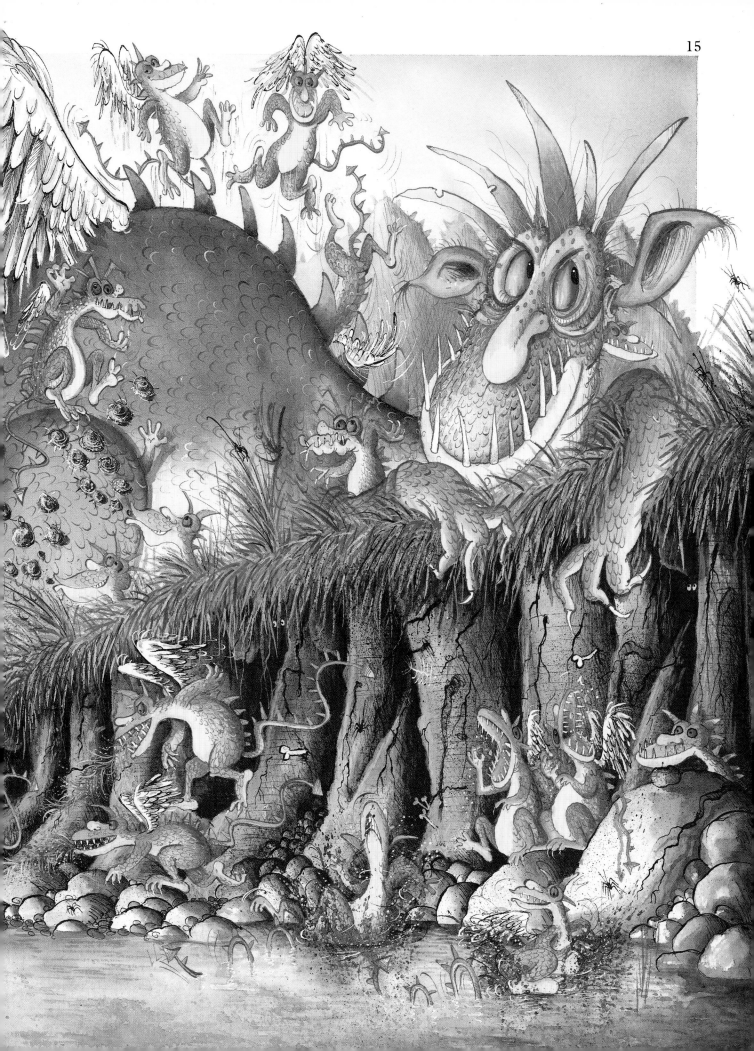

The School for Young Dragons

At the school for young dragons
The main lessons are
Flying and feasting and fighting.

In flying they learn
How to take off and land
How to dive and to swoop
How to loop the loop
And how to leave trails of sky-writing.

In feasting they learn
About how to behave
When invited to dine
In an old dragon's cave.
They learn that it's rude
To gobble your food,
That you should not belch fire
That you must always sit up straight
And never, ever, scorch your plate.

In fighting they learn
How to scare off their foes
With jets of flame
That will singe their toes,
How to puff a smoke screen
So they cannot be seen.
How a knight with a lance
Hasn't much of a chance
Against dragons who know
How a whack of the tail
Can shatter chain-mail.

At the school for young dragons
The main lessons are
Flying and feasting and fighting,
Which is why you will hear
A young dragon say
'Our lessons are really exciting!
It's better than reading and writing!'

John Foster

SCHOOL
FOR YOUNG
DRAGONS
NO KNIGHTS

Never Trust Dragons

'I see you've arrived,' the dragon said,
bright eyes like beacons set in his head.

'Yes,' said the vet. 'Left as soon as I knew.
Now tell me the problem, a touch of the 'flu?'

'My flame has gone out, I can't raise a spark,
not much use when you hunt in the dark.'

The vet peered down the gigantic throat,
black as a chimney and reeking of soot.

He threw in some petrol, a match to ignite,
firelighters, coal, and some dynamite.

The dragon covered a burp with his paw,
a flicker of flame flashed down his jaw.

He licked his lips with a golden tongue:
'Take your fee, vet, you'd better run.

I can feel my fires boil, they are returning.
In a couple of minutes you could be burning.'

Clutching a diamond the size of a star,
the vet scampered away to his car.

As he drove off the dragon's bright fires
gushed out of the cave and scorched his tyres.

The vet snapped his fingers, laughed at the brute
because he was wearing his flame-proof suit.

David Harmer

Lost and Found

LOST:
A Wizard's loving pet.
Rather longish.
Somewhat scaly.
May be hungry or
upset.
Please feed daily.

P. S. Reward.

FOUND:
A dragon
breathing fire.
Flails his scaly
tail
in ire.
Would eat twenty LARGE meals
daily
if we let him.
Please
come and get him.

P. S. No reward necessary.

Lilian Moore

Anyone Wanting a Fiery Dragon?

With a sulphur smell,
The air grew hot
As the dragon steamed
On the used car lot.

'Genuine scales,
A spiky tail,'
The notice said,
'This beast for sale.'

'Belches flame
In a crimson sheet,
And guarantees
A steady heat.'

'Huge and fearless,
Brave and bold
And thermostatically
Controlled.'

'It's careful not
To sear or scorch.
Use as a heater
Or a torch.'

'Warmer than
A blacksmith's forge,
And recommended
By Saint George.'

I bought the beast,
What else to do?
Now you should see
My barbecue!

Max Fatchen

The Toaster

A silver-scaled Dragon with jaws flaming red
Sits at my elbow and toasts my bread.
I hand him fat slices, and then, one by one,
He hands them back when he sees they are done.

William Jay Smith

Drawback

The dragon raged with flame and fire,
He blew it down his nose –
But the poor old soul was quite cross-eyed
And burnt off all his toes.

Clive Webster

Dragon Band

It's the best in the land,
The Dragon Band:
There's **Gnorda**
On recorder,
Gondar
On guitar,
Dronga
On the bonger
And the big Oompah;
Dorgan
Plays the organ,
And **Ardong**
Sings a song
(It does drag on a bit,
It's much too long!)
G. Darno plays piano,
Giving it a bash;
And **Randgo**
Twangs a banjo
With great panache.
When they get it
All together
It's grand, **O grand!**
It's the latest,
It's the greatest,
It's the Dragon Band!

Eric Finney

Is there a Dragon in the House?

I visited a castle
One summer afternoon.
I didn't want to join the crowd,
So I wandered off alone
Over the creaking drawbridge
Past the tower keep,
And in a courtyard
On the cobbles
I came upon a Dragon –
Yes, a Dragon –
Fast asleep.

I could see that it was sleeping
And not a ghost or dead,
For I saw it gently breathing
And it flicked its heavy ears
Against the flies that buzzed its head.

I tiptoed up to touch it
For curiosity
And proof.
And its scales were rough as the bark of a tree
And thick as tiles on a roof.

Then the crowd came round the corner
And the crowd's guide said,
'And it's here in this very courtyard
That a Knight fought a terrible Dragon
And the Dragon dropped down dead.'

The Dragon opened yellow eyes,
It yawned and stretched and blinked,
And over the heads of the guide and crowd
It looked
At me
And winked.

'Oh, no. Not dead,'
The Dragon said,
'That isn't Dragon lore.'
But no one else there heard it speak,
No one else there saw.

'As sure as grass is green,'
The Dragon said,
'As sure as daisies grow,
Dragons do not die,
They simply come and go.
They come and go as surely
As heroes in tin will dent.'
Then it grinned and waved its tail
And then the Dragon
Went.

The crowd moved on behind the guide
Through a narrow castle door.
They clattered, scuffed and tripped
The cobbled courtyard floor,
But none of those feet
Rubbed out the print,
The print of the Dragon's paw.

The print of its paw
On the cobbles
Left behind to show
That Dragons do not die
They simply come and go.

This story is for Dragons,
For I've never thought it right
That Dragons should be invented
To make a hero of a Knight.

Julie Holder

The Grateful Dragon

A dragon crawled to the castle door
   and everyone inside
looked down on it from the castle walls,
   curious but terrified.

It was half the size of a football pitch,
   bright green, with spots of red,
but it hadn't the strength to lash its tail
   and lay there, as if dead.

The Winter had turned the woods to iron,
   the snow was deep as a house;
there wasn't a blade of grass to be seen
   nor a skinny harvest mouse.

'It's starving!' the King cried. 'Now's our chance!' –
   looking down from the castle wall –
'Bring lances and crossbows and arrows
   and let's kill it, once for all.'

The dragon was too weak to move
   more than an eyelid, and yet
the Princess saw a tear form there and it
   moved her heart with regret.

'Please spare the dragon!' the Princess begged.
    'Put out some bundles of hay.
Once it's grown strong from eating it will
    harmlessly go away.'

The King looked hard in his daughter's face
    and saw how much she cared,
then nodded that they should do as she asked,
    and so the dragon was spared.

Next Autumn brought enemy soldiers.
    The King and his subjects shut
themselves in the castle, and there they starved
    while the harvest stayed uncut.

The Princess wept on the castle wall
    when suddenly there came
in a whirlwind of thunder and fury
    the dragon, spouting flame.

The enemy soldiers ran off in fright
    and never again were seen;
and the people came out of the castle
    and gathered the harvest in.

Raymond Wilson

The Lonely Dragon

He lives in the mouth of a mountain
Behind the teeth of mist,
He sighs at the thought
Of the Knights he's not fought
And the maidens he never has kissed.

He sprawls in a nest of treasure,
Plays fivestones with rubies and pearls.
On the back of his paw he wipes his nose,
And idly on his rattling toes
The crown of a King he twirls.

He belches and scratches his belly,
He is bored with before and behind him.
He spits sparks to the dark and sings rude songs,
His roars shake the mountain tops like blancmange,
But only the spiders mind him.

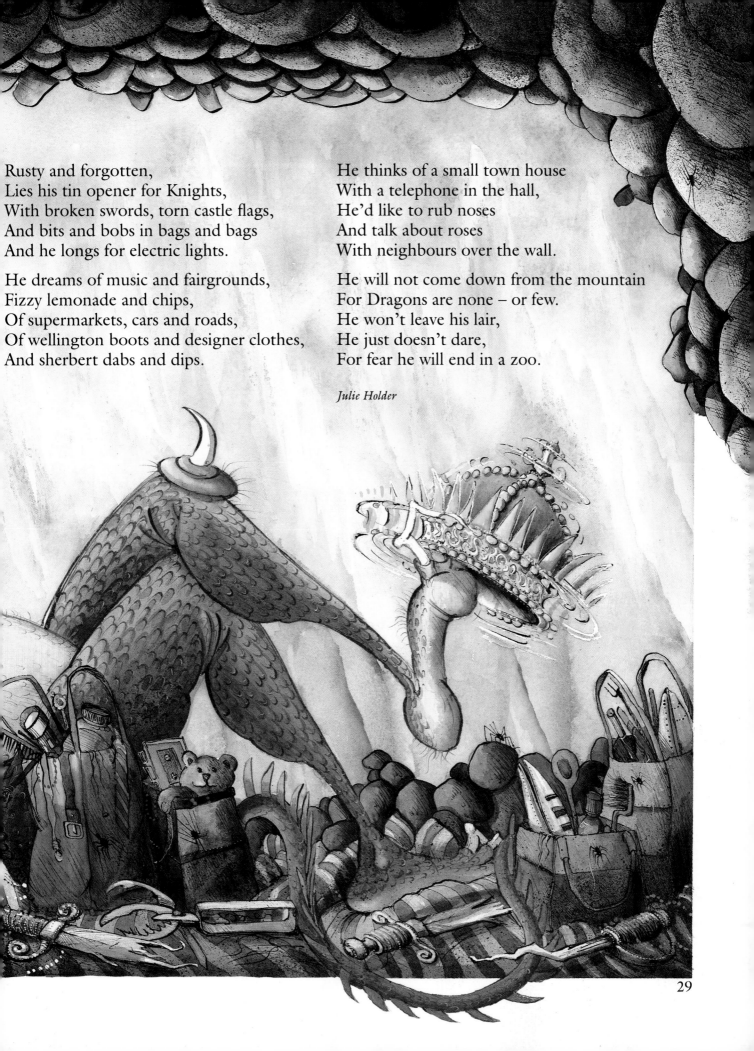

Rusty and forgotten,
Lies his tin opener for Knights,
With broken swords, torn castle flags,
And bits and bobs in bags and bags
And he longs for electric lights.

He dreams of music and fairgrounds,
Fizzy lemonade and chips,
Of supermarkets, cars and roads,
Of wellington boots and designer clothes,
And sherbert dabs and dips.

He thinks of a small town house
With a telephone in the hall,
He'd like to rub noses
And talk about roses
With neighbours over the wall.

He will not come down from the mountain
For Dragons are none – or few.
He won't leave his lair,
He just doesn't dare,
For fear he will end in a zoo.

Julie Holder

The Dragon

I saw a cloud like a dragon,
Lying in wait in the sky,
With a purple head and a purple tail
And a little blue patch for an eye.

From his snout came flames of fire,
And he began to run,
Chasing the daylight away to the west
And fighting the setting sun!

Daphne Lister

The Ice Dragons

They tell of Polar dragons
Who breathe frost instead of fire,
With icicles nine along their backs,
Each one a glassy spire.
In the eerie light
Of that endless white
Where bleak winds always blow,
They make their homes
Neath icy domes
In everlasting snow.
And when these dragons gather
(This is the tale that's told)
They stand in an Arctic Circle,
They breathe,
And the world grows cold.

Eric Finney

The Last Dragon

Beneath a high mountain,
Inside a dark cave,
A crusty old dragon,
As cold as the grave.

As cold as the high,
Vaulted stone overhead.
As cold as the gold
That is spilled as his bed.

The last of the dragons.
There will be no more.
And slow beats his heart
On his glittering store.

The beating gets slower
As life drifts away.
A hundred more lifetimes
Just pass as a day.

At last a low moan
Where there once was a roar.
The last of the dragons
Is breathing no more.

Ian Larmont

John Foster and Korky Paul
DINOSAUR
POEMS

Oxford University Press

Oxford New York Toronto

Acknowledgements

The editor and publisher are grateful for permission to include the following copyright material.

Tony Bradman, 'At the Museum'. © 1993 Tony Bradman. Reprinted by permission of Rogers, Coleridge, & White Ltd.

John Cotton, 'The Bookoceros or Ancient Thesaurus'. © 1993 John Cotton. Reprinted by permission of the author.

Max Fatchen, 'Who's There?'. © 1993 Max Fatchen. Reprinted by permission of John Johnson (Authors' Agent) Ltd.

John Foster, 'Ten Dancing Dinosaurs'. © 1993 John Foster. Reprinted by permission of the author.

David Harmer, 'Dinosaur Stomp' from *My Blue Poetry Book* (Macmillan Educational), edited Moira Andrew. Reprinted by permission of the author.

Trevor Harvey, 'At the Dinosaurs' Party'. © 1993 Trevor Harvey. Reprinted by permission of the author.

Gail Kredenser, 'Brontosaurus'. © Gail Kredenser. Used with permission.

Wendy Larmont, 'Stegosaurus'. © 1993 Wendy Larmont. Reprinted by permission of the author.

Doug MacLeod, 'Ode to an Extinct Dinosaur' from *In the Garden of Bad Things*. Reprinted by permission of Penguin Books Australia Ltd as publisher.

Wes Magee, 'Tyrannosaurus Rex'. © Wes Magee. Reprinted by permission of the author.

Trevor Millum, 'A Stegosaurus is for life'. © 1993 Trevor Millum. Reprinted by permission of the author.

Brian Moses, 'Trouble at the Dinosaur Café'. © 1993 Brian Moses. Reprinted by permission of the author.

Judith Nicholls, 'Dinosauristory', first published in *Popcorn Pie* by Judith Nicholls (Mary Glasgow Publications), © Judith Nicholls 1988. Reprinted by permission of the author.

Jack Prelutsky, 'Ankylosaurus' from *Tyrannosaurus Was a Beast*. Text © 1988 by Jack Prelutsky. Published in the UK by Walker Books Limited and reprinted with their permission. Published in the USA by Wm Morrow & Co. Inc.

Irene Rawnsley, 'James and the Dinosaur'. © 1993 Irene Rawnsley. Reprinted by permission of the author.

Charles Thomson, 'My Pet Dinosaur' from *I'm Brilliant* (Collins Book Bus). Reprinted by permission of the author and Collins Educational Publ.

Clive Webster, 'Companion' and 'Problem Solved' both © 1993 Clive Webster. Reprinted by permission of the author.

Martyn Wiley, 'When the Dinosaur Came to Stay'. © 1993 Martyn Wiley. Reprinted by permission of the author.

Raymond Wilson, 'The Big Con'. © 1993 Raymond Wilson. Reprinted by permission of the author.

We may have failed in some instances to contact the copyright holder. If notified, the publisher will be pleased to make necessary corrections in future editions.

For Angus Hamilton Gordon   K.P.

Oxford University Press, Great Clarendon Street, Oxford OX2 6DP
Oxford New York
Athens Auckland Bangkok Bogota Bombay
Buenos Aires Calcutta Cape Town Dar es Salaam
Delhi Florence Hong Kong Istanbul Karachi
Kuala Lumpur Madras Madrid Melbourne
Mexico City Nairobi Paris Singapore
Taipei Tokyo Toronto Warsaw
and associated companies in
Berlin Ibadan

Oxford is a trade mark of Oxford University Press

This selection and arrangement © John Foster 1993
Illustrations © Korky Paul 1993
First published 1993
First published in paperback 1994
Reprinted in paperback 1994, 1995 (twice), 1998
First published in this hardback edition 1998

ISBN 0 19 276126 9 (paperback)
ISBN 0 19 276195 1 (composite)

A CIP catalogue record for this book is available from the British Library

Set by Pentacor PLC, High Wycombe, Bucks
Printed in Hong Kong

CONTENTS

Companion

I have an allosaurus
And I take him everywhere,
And really I can't understand
Why people stop and stare.

He's loving, kind and gentle,
He wouldn't hurt a soul,
Unless of course you laughed at him—
And then he'd eat you whole!

Clive Webster

4

Dinosaur Stomp

I thought I saw
a Dinosaur
buy a pair of slippers
in a big shoe-store
I asked him what
he bought them for
and he told me
his paw was sore
and what's more
began to roar
and showed me what
his teeth were for.

I ran like mad
across the floor
and bolted through
the shoe-store door
and nevermore
no nevermore
laughed out loud
at a Dinosaur.

David Harmer

5

Ten Dancing Dinosaurs

Ten dancing dinosaurs in a chorus line
One fell and split her skirt, then there were nine.

Nine dancing dinosaurs at a village fête
One was raffled as a prize, then there were eight.

Seven dancing dinosaurs performing magic tricks
One did a vanishing act, then there were six.

Six dancing dinosaurs
Learning how to jive

Four dancing dinosaurs waltzing in the sea
A mermaid kidnapped one, then there were three.

Three dancing dinosaurs head-banging in a zo
One knocked himself out, then there were two

Eight dancing dinosaurs on a pier in Devon
One fell overboard, then there were seven.

One got twisted in a knot,
Then there were five.

Five dancing dinosaurs gyrating on the floor
One crashed through the floorboards, then there were four.

wo dancing dinosaurs rocking round the sun
ne collapsed from sunstroke, then there was one.

One dancing dinosaur hijacked a plane
Flew off to Alaska and was never seen again.

John Foster

7

Stegosaurus

I have a stegosaurus
He's really rather sweet.
But he's very, very fussy
About the food he'll eat.

I offered him a burger,
A plate of egg and chips,
A dish of chicken curry,
But none would pass his lips.

I asked, 'What would be tasty?
I'll get it if I can.'
He said, 'I'd better tell you . . .
I'm a VEGETARIAN!'

Wendy Larmont

Dinosauristory

Hocus, pocus,
plodding through the swamp;
I'm a diplodocus,
chomp, chomp, chomp!
Grass for breakfast,
I could eat a tree!
Grass for lunch and dinner
and grass for tea.
I'm a diplodocus
plodding through the swamp,
hocus-rocus pocus,
chomp, chomp, chomp!

Judith Nicholls

Tyrannosaurus Rex
(the King of the tyrant lizards)

Two daft little arms like toasting forks,
enough skin to make coats for ten men.
    As dirty as pitch
      (he slept rough in a ditch),
and the feet from a monstrous hen.

A bit of a freak—part beast, part bird.
Would you dare stick your tongue out at him?
    He's a mean dinosaur
      with a mouth wide as a door
and teeth that stand up dagger-slim.

Across the mud flats he belts in top gear;
a rogue lighthouse with blood on his brain.
    Better kneel down and pray
      for all those in his way:
he'll grind bones again and again.

Wes Magee

10

Ankylosaurus

Clankity Clankity Clankity Clank!
Ankylosaurus was built like a tank,
its hide was a fortress as sturdy as steel,
it tended to be an inedible meal.

It was armoured in front, it was armoured behind,
there wasn't a thing on its miniscule mind,
it waddled about on its four stubby legs,
nibbling on plants with a mouthful of pegs.

Ankylosaurus was best left alone,
its tail was a cudgel of gristle and bone,
Clankity Clankity Clankity Clank!
Ankylosaurus was built like a tank.

Jack Prelutsky

11

Ode to an Extinct Dinosaur

Iguanadon, I loved you,
With all your spiky scales,
Your massive jaws,
Impressive claws
And teeth like horseshoe nails.

Iguanadon, I loved you.
It moved me close to tears
When first I read
That you've been dead
For ninety million years.

Doug Macleod

The Bookoceros or Ancient Thesaurus

The Thesaurus has a ravenous appetite
From any passing page he will take a bite.
As for dictionaries and such
He eats them for breakfast
He likes them so much.

Nouns are his staple as you would guess
Though he's not averse to a well-cooked mess
Of a porridge of paragraphs containing long words,
But he prefers prepositions with a few stewed verbs.

If he should over-eat, what will he do?
He will just cough up a sentence or two!

John Cotton

13

The Big Con

Brontosaurus, Stegosaurus, whatever the name;
Tyrannosaurus, Spinosaurus, it's one and the same—
They clubbed together, one and all,
To make the rest of us look *small!*

As long as a cricket pitch, snout to tail,
With tree-trunk legs and plated mail,
Snarling like thunder, and humped like a hill,
They could eat a whole haystack and be hungry still.

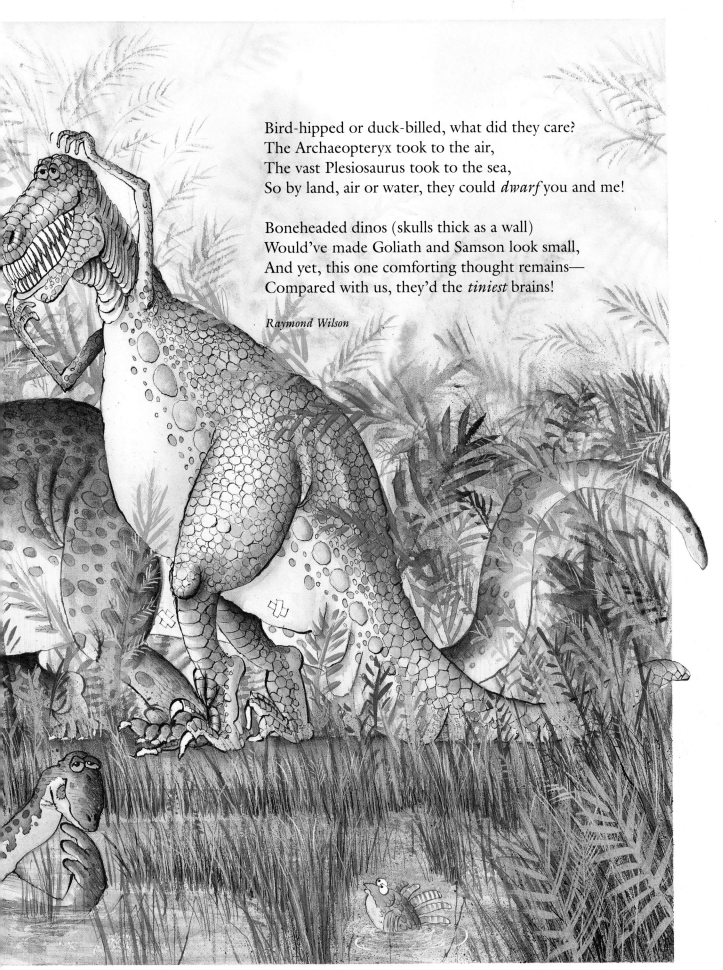

Bird-hipped or duck-billed, what did they care?
The Archaeopteryx took to the air,
The vast Plesiosaurus took to the sea,
So by land, air or water, they could *dwarf* you and me!

Boneheaded dinos (skulls thick as a wall)
Would've made Goliath and Samson look small,
And yet, this one comforting thought remains—
Compared with us, they'd the *tiniest* brains!

Raymond Wilson

Brontosaurus

The giant brontosaurus
Was a prehistoric chap
With four fat feet to stand on
And a very skimpy lap.
The scientists assure us
Of a most amazing thing—
A brontosaurus blossomed
When he had a chance to sing!

(The bigger brontosauruses,
Who liked to sing in choruses,
Would close their eyes and harmonize
And sing most anything.)

They growled and they yowled,
They deedled and they dummed;
They warbled and they whistled,
They howled and they hummed.
They didn't eat, they didn't sleep;
They sang and sang all day.
Now all you'll find are footprints
Where they tapped the time away!

Gail Kredenser

16

At the Dinosaurs' Party

At the dinosaurs' party
They had a great time—
They played HEAVY ROCK
And then ROLLED in the slime!

They kept a GOOD BEAT
With a SWISH of the tail,
As they ROARED up and down
The REPTILEAN scale!

At the dinosaurs' party
They SHOOK the whole earth—
As they RANTED and RAVED
For ALL THEY WERE WORTH!

Trevor Harvey

Trouble at the Dinosaur Café

Down at the dinosaur café
everybody was doing fine.
Steggy was slurping swamp juice
while Iggy sat down to dine.

Bronto was eating his tree-roots
and had ordered vegetable pie,
when in stomped Tyrannosaurus
with a wicked gleam in his eye.

He read the menu from left to right
then gobbled it up in one gulp.
He chewed upon it thoughtfully
while the paper turned to pulp.

'You plant eaters are fine,' he said,
'if that's all you want to eat.
But I'm a growing dinosaur
and my stomach cries out for meat.'

'I need something extra
to see me through my day.
I do lots of ROARING and BELLOWING,
I just can't get by on hay.'

Steggy stiffened, Iggy trembled,
while Bronto fell off his chair.
Tyrannosaurus turned his head
and fixed him with his stare.

'There's nothing I like more,' he said,
'than a tasty dinosaur stew,
and for extra special flavour
I'll add YOU and YOU and YOU . . . !'

Brian Moses

19

When the Dinosaur Came to Stay

Monday; he got stuck in the bath.
We had to get a crane
To pull him out.

Tuesday; he sat on the settee
It broke into a thousand bits
Mum shouted at him.

Wednesday; he went into the garden
Ate all the roses
Then started chewing the lawn.

Thursday; he helped in the kitchen
Peeled three tons of potatoes
Then pulled the taps off the wall.

Friday; the water was two metres deep
So he sucked it out of the house
Sprayed it down the street.

Saturday; he went home, caught a bus
Picked it up in one hand, had a look inside
Then caught the train instead.

Martyn Wiley

21

My Dinosaur's Day in the Park

My pet dinosaur got in trouble
When we went for a walk in the park.
I took off his leash and let him run free.
He didn't come back until dark.
He ate up the new row of oak trees
(The gardener was fit to be tied).
Then he stopped in the playground and bent down his head
And the kids used his neck for a slide.

He knocked down the fence by the boat pond
With a swing of his twenty-foot tail;
When he stopped to explain he was sorry,
His legs blocked the bicycle trail.

When the sun set, my dino got worried;
He's always been scared of the dark.
He sat down on the ground and started to cry,
His tears flooded out the whole park.
A friend of mine rowed his boat over
When he heard of my pet dino's sad roar.
He showed him the way home to my house
And helped him unlock the front door.

He's a lovable, lumbering fellow
But after my pet had his spree,
They put up a sign in the park and it reads
NO DINOS ALLOWED TO RUN FREE.

Elizabeth Winthrop Mahoney

23

A Stegosaurus is for Life

Down in a fern-decked valley
Far from the sun's fierce glare,
A smiling stegosaurus
Laid her eggs with loving care.

But so as to protect them
From tyrannosaurus rex,
She thought, *I'll dig a little hole*
And cover up these eggs.

The soil around was rich and moist;
The hole she dug was deep.
The fine pink eggs they huddled there,
As if they were asleep.

Now Mrs Steg was charming
And kind to all she met
But she had one tiny little fault:
She was likely to forget.

So time went by and seasons passed,
An ice-age came and went.
The eggs lay frozen in the earth
Near Tenterden in Kent.

One day a yellow JCB
Laying pipelines for some gas,
Dug up five strange pink objects
And laid them in the grass.

X Y and Zeddy saw them;
They took them home as toys
And in the middle of the night
They heard a tapping noise.

At first a claw crept through the crack
Fast followed by a snout,
A head and then a body
As a grey green . . . *thing* hatched out.

The children were delighted;
They took them out for walks.
They fed them on bananas
And dandelion stalks.

The children grew up slowly:
The stegosauri grew up fast.
Their tails all sprouted deadly spikes
And their bony plates were vast.

'They'll have to go!' said grown-ups,
'To Science Lab—or zoo—
It might be to a circus—
It's really up to you.'

WANTED: good home for a reptile.
As watchdogs they're the best;
They'll baby-sit for hours
And stamp on household pests;
Make all your neighbours jealous
Of your rockeries on legs
They'll scare a burglar silly
And may even lay you eggs!

Trevor Millum

My Pet Dinosaur

My dinosaur
was getting thinner
and so I brought him
home for dinner.

He ate as fast
as he was able:
he ate the food,
he ate the table.

He ate the fridge,
he ate the chair,
he ate my favourite
teddy bear.

He is a very
naughty pet.
He even ate
the TV set.

Charles Thomson

Who's There?

If you hear a dinosaur
Knocking loudly on your door,
Through the keyhole firmly say
'Nobody is home today'.
If the bell should start to ring,
Tell the beast, 'No visiting'.
If you see there's more than one,
Turn around and start to run.

Max Fatchen

At the Museum

I was an ancient dinosaur
  I lived so long ago;
I walked through steaming jungles
  And my gait was very slow.

I ate the juicy fern plants
  And I wallowed in the mud;
I loved to lie out in the sun
  And feel it warm my blood.

I splashed along the sea-shore
  I squelched in muddy swamps,
And when I crossed the boiling plains
  My feet went . . .
STOMP! STOMP STOMP!

My giant footsteps shook the Earth,
  My shadow terrified
The tiny, waiting creatures
  Who watched me as I died.

I was a meal for others
  As the skin fell from my bones . . .
A hundred million years went by.
  My bones turned into stone.

A fossil remnant I became,
 Some bones locked in the land,
And there I stayed till I was freed
 And cleaned by human hands.

My bones were put together
 To make a fine display,
And you can come to look at me
 Almost every day.

Come closer . . . can you feel it?
 It's the jungle's steaming heat.
And now the ground starts shaking
 As I walk with giant feet.

See the fern trees parting
 As thunderous and slow
I come looking for my dinner . . .
 But that was long ago.

I was an ancient dinosaur,
 But now you find me here;
A message that's been waiting
 For a hundred million years.

Tony Bradman

29

James and the Dinosaur

At the Museum
when the keeper couldn't see him
James climbed inside the bones
of a dinosaur.

Up its tail
through the rib rings
James explored its crevices
put his head into the skull,
imagining.

Quick heart
hot breath
such questionings inside him
made the bones of the dinosaur
erupt from death.

He tore at his moorings
pushed aside the keeper
broke from the stares
of the people come to see;
smashed through the wall
with James riding inside him
crashed into the street
to be free.

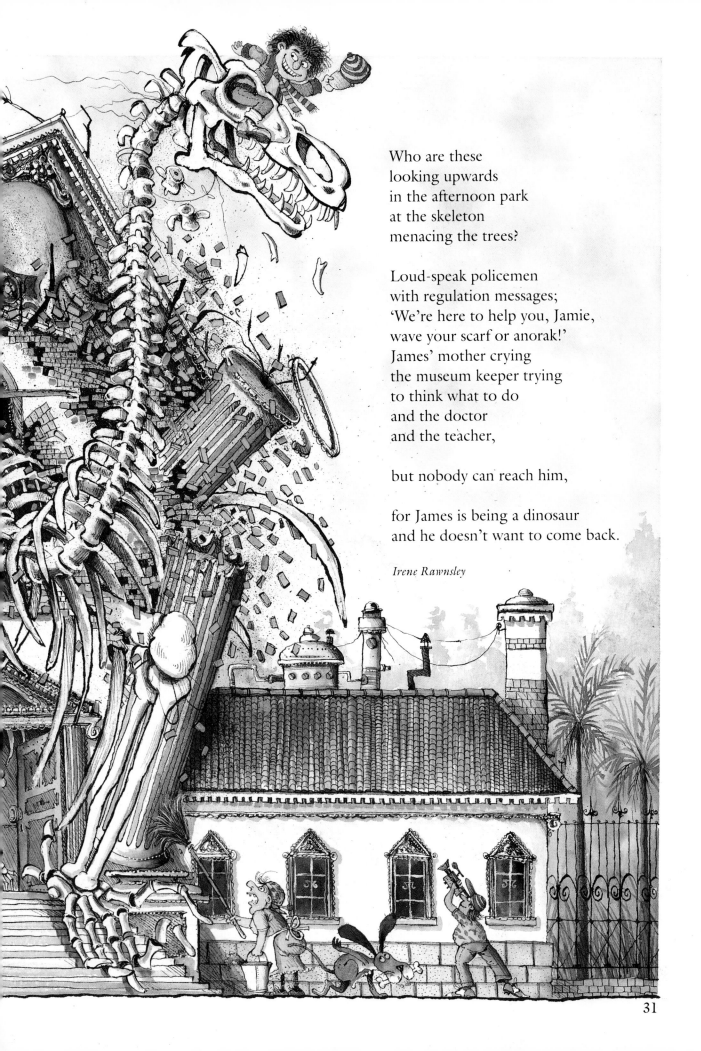

Who are these
looking upwards
in the afternoon park
at the skeleton
menacing the trees?

Loud-speak policemen
with regulation messages;
'We're here to help you, Jamie,
wave your scarf or anorak!'
James' mother crying
the museum keeper trying
to think what to do
and the doctor
and the teacher,

but nobody can reach him,

for James is being a dinosaur
and he doesn't want to come back.

Irene Rawnsley

Problem Solved

Our teacher says it's a mystery
Why dinosaurs died long ago.
They just disappeared
After millions of years
And why, we may well never know.

But I've got a theory about it—
They didn't just run out of breath.
Like us they had schools
With lessons and rules
And the teachers just bored them to death.

Clive Webster

John Foster and Korky Paul

MONSTER
POEMS

Oxford University Press
Oxford   New York   Toronto

Acknowledgements

The editor and publisher are grateful for permission to include the following poems:

Michael Baldwin, 'The Truth about the Abominable Footprint', © 1995 Michael Baldwin. Reprinted by permission of the author.

Paul Cookson, 'It', © 1995 Paul Cookson. Reprinted by permission of the author.

Richard Edwards, 'Three of a Kind', from *The House That Caught a Cold* (Viking, 1991); 'The Sliver-Slurk', from *A Mouse in my Roof* (Orchard Books, 1988); and 'The Last Monster', © 1995 Richard Edwards. All reprinted by permission of the author.

Eric Finney, 'The Night of the Junk Monsters', © 1995 Eric Finney. Reprinted by permission of the author.

John Foster, 'The Snow Monster' and 'The Fire Monster', © 1995 John Foster. Reprinted by permission of the author.

David Harmer, 'Watch Your Teacher Carefully', © 1995 David Harmer. Reprinted by permission of the author.

Julie Holder, 'The Alien' and 'The Monster Behind the Loo', © 1995 Julie Holder. Reprinted by permission of the author.

Robin Mellor, 'The Glamdrak', © 1995 Robin Mellor. Reprinted by permission of the author.

Trevor Millum, 'Tell Me It Isn't', © 1990 Trevor Millum, first published in *The Usborne Book of Creepy Poems*, edited by Heather Amery (1990). Reprinted by permission of the author.

Michaela Morgan, 'Question Time' and 'Be Wary of the Werewolf Wild', © 1995 Michaela Morgan. Reprinted by permission of the author.

Brian Morse, 'Get You', © 1995 Brian Morse. Reprinted by permission of the author.

Brian Moses, 'The Grumposaurus' from *Hippopotamus Dancing* (CUP, 1994). Reprinted by permission of the author, and Cambridge University Press.

Judith Nicholls, 'Make Your Own Monster: A DIY Guide', © 1995 Judith Nicholls. Reprinted by permission of the author.

Jack Prelutsky, 'Help', from *The Snopp on the Sidewalk*, © 1976, 1977 by Jack Prelutsky. Reprinted by permission of Greenwillow Books, a division of William Morrow & Company, Inc. 'The Underwater Wibbles' from *The New Kid on the Block*, © 1984 by Jack Prelutsky (published in the UK by Wm Heinemann and in the USA by Greenwillow). Reprinted by permission of Reed Consumer Books and Greenwillow Books, a division of William Morrow & Company, Inc.

Rowena Sommerville, 'The Monster's Heart', © 1995 Rowena Sommerville. Reprinted by permission of the author.

Clive Webster, 'Mistaken Identity' and 'Epitaph for Frankenstein', © 1995 Clive Webster. Reprinted by permission of the author.

For Paul Hamilton Christie Gordon. K.P.

Oxford University Press, Great Clarendon Street, Oxford OX2 6DP
Oxford New York
Athens Auckland Bangkok Bogota Bombay
Buenos Aires Calcutta Cape Town Dar es Salaam
Delhi Florence Hong Kong Istanbul Karachi
Kuala Lumpur Madras Madrid Melbourne
Mexico City Nairobi Paris Singapore
Taipei Tokyo Toronto Warsaw
and associated companies in
Berlin Ibadan

Oxford is a trade mark of Oxford University Press

This selection and arrangement © John Foster 1995
Illustrations © Korky Paul 1995

First published 1995
First published in this hardback edition 1998

A CIP catalogue record for this book is available from the British Library
ISBN 0 19 276140 4 (hardback)
ISBN 0 19 276147 1 (paperback)
ISBN 0 19 276195 1 (composite)

Printed in Hong Kong

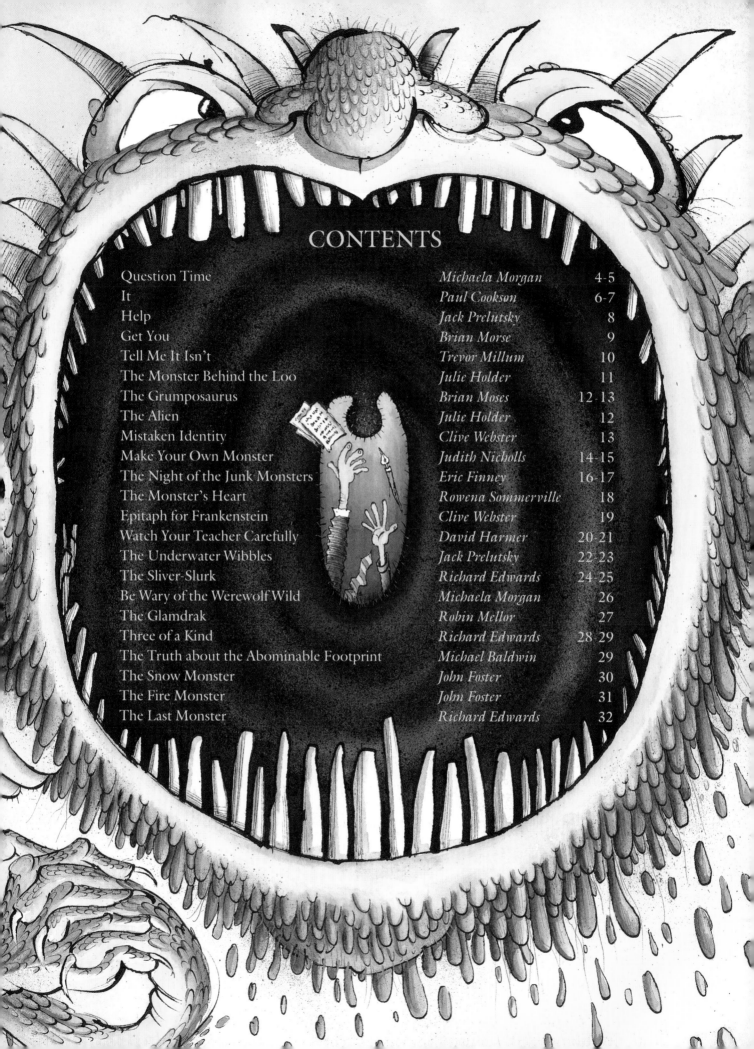

CONTENTS

Question Time

WHAT DOES A MONSTER LOOK LIKE?

Well . . . hairy
and scary,
and furry
and burly and pimply and dimply and warty and naughty and wrinkled and
crinkled . . .
That's what a monster looks like.

HOW DOES A MONSTER MOVE?

It oozes,
it shambles,
it crawls and it ambles, it slouches and shuffles and trudges, it lumbers
and toddles, it creeps and it waddles . . .
That's how a monster moves.

WHERE DOES A MONSTER LIVE?

In garden sheds,
under beds,
in wardrobes, in plug holes and ditches,
beneath city streets, just under your feet . . .
That's where a monster lives.

HOW DOES A MONSTER EAT?

It slurps and it burps and gobbles and gulps and sips and swallows and
scoffs, it nibbles and munches, it chews and it crunches . . .
That's how a monster eats.

WHAT DOES A MONSTER EAT?

Slugs and bats and bugs and rats and stones and mud and bones and blood
and squelchy squids . . . and nosy kids.
YUM!
That's what a monster eats!

Michaela Morgan

5

It

It hides inside your wardrobe.
It hides beneath your bed.
Sometimes Its eyes are yellow
And sometimes they are red.
It makes those spooky noises
That no one else can hear
And when you're fast asleep
It whispers in your ear.
It has ten thousand teeth
And eats your underwear
And when you try and find your vest
It's never ever there.
It has a great big hairy nose
That's full of boils and spots
But doesn't seem to smell a thing
Because It eats your socks.
It hides your favourite toys
And breaks your favourite game.
It colours on your favourite book
And you get all the blame.
It stops you doing homework
And switches on the telly.
It forces you to eat up all
The chocolate cake and jelly.

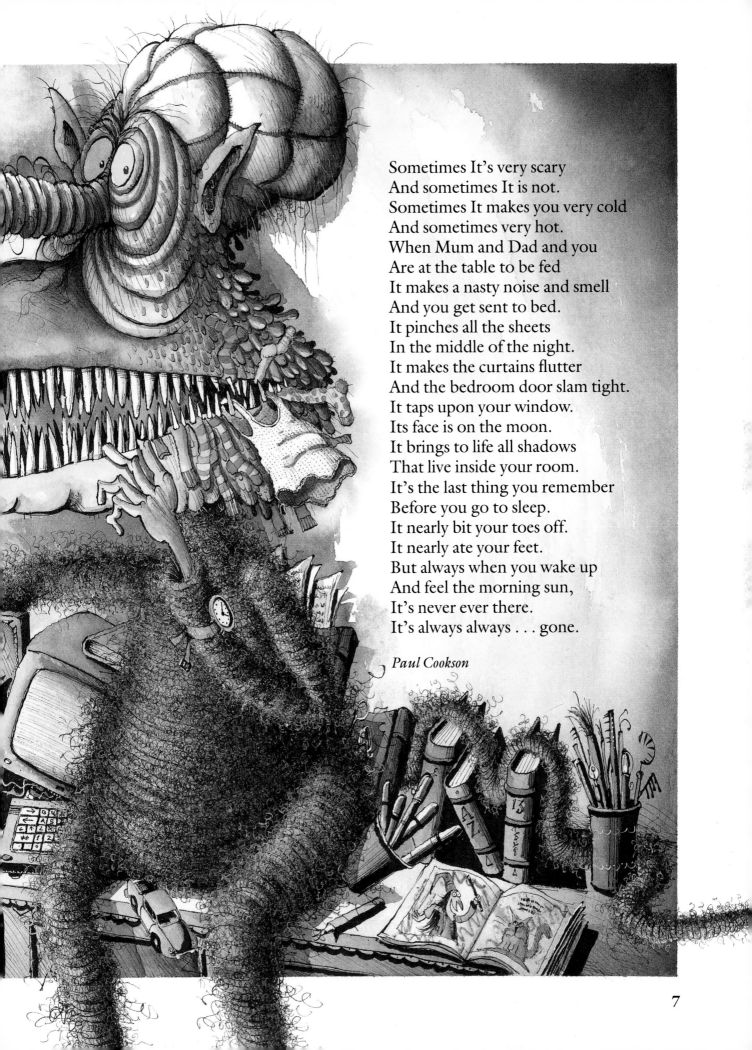

Sometimes It's very scary
And sometimes It is not.
Sometimes It makes you very cold
And sometimes very hot.
When Mum and Dad and you
Are at the table to be fed
It makes a nasty noise and smell
And you get sent to bed.
It pinches all the sheets
In the middle of the night.
It makes the curtains flutter
And the bedroom door slam tight.
It taps upon your window.
Its face is on the moon.
It brings to life all shadows
That live inside your room.
It's the last thing you remember
Before you go to sleep.
It nearly bit your toes off.
It nearly ate your feet.
But always when you wake up
And feel the morning sun,
It's never ever there.
It's always always . . . gone.

Paul Cookson

7

Help

Can anybody tell me, please,
a bit about the thing
with seven legs and furry knees,
four noses and a wing?

Oh, what has prickles on its chin,
what's yellow, green, and blue,
and what has soft and slimy skin?
Oh, tell me, tell me, do.

And tell me, what has polka dots
on every other ear,
what ties its tail in twenty knots,
what weeps a purple tear?

Oh, what is growling long and low
and please, has it been fed?
I think I'd really better know . . .
it's sitting on my head.

Jack Prelutsky

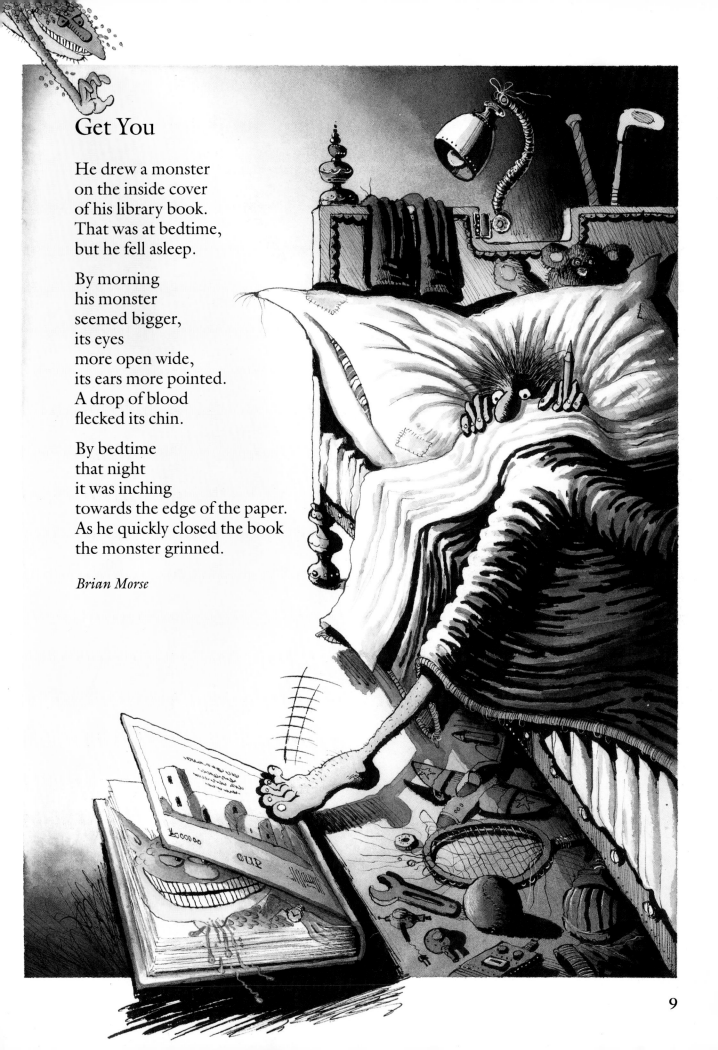

Get You

He drew a monster
on the inside cover
of his library book.
That was at bedtime,
but he fell asleep.

By morning
his monster
seemed bigger,
its eyes
more open wide,
its ears more pointed.
A drop of blood
flecked its chin.

By bedtime
that night
it was inching
towards the edge of the paper.
As he quickly closed the book
the monster grinned.

Brian Morse

9

Tell Me It Isn't!

Try not to stare
But tell me — that shadow there
With its head in the air
It isn't a bear . . .
There *isn't* a bear
Come out of its lair
At the top of the stair
Is there?

Take care how you speak,
But tell me, that creak,
It isn't the creak of the freak
The flying freak
With the crooked beak
About to sneak
Up from behind
IS it?

Tell me, that sound
Isn't the sound of the hound
The red-eyed hound
Creeping around
Dribbling and crunching
The bones it found
About to leap with one bound
On my back! *It isn't, is it?*

Tell me, that movement I saw
Behind the door
It wasn't a paw
Wasn't a claw
It wasn't the Beast
About to roar
And pounce and gnaw —
WAS IT?

Yes, I know you told me before
But I'm still not sure
So, tell me *once* more.

Trevor Millum

10

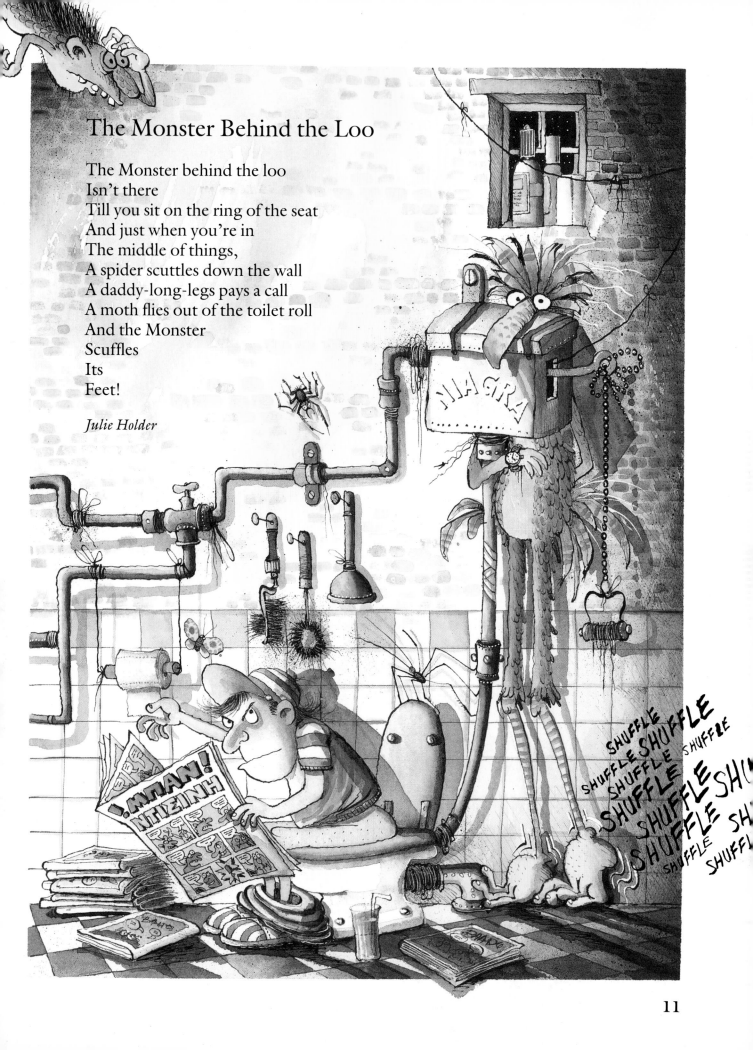

The Monster Behind the Loo

The Monster behind the loo
Isn't there
Till you sit on the ring of the seat
And just when you're in
The middle of things,
A spider scuttles down the wall
A daddy-long-legs pays a call
A moth flies out of the toilet roll
And the Monster
Scuffles
Its
Feet!

Julie Holder

11

The Grumposaurus

Each morning a grumposaurus
tears into our bedroom,
she burrows down
beneath the duvet
and roars out commands
most grumposaurusly:
'Where's my drink?'
'I want a story!'

We really have to take care
not to annoy this beast,
give her milk and cereal,
a TV cartoon or two.
Then at times the grumposaurus
can be quite friendly,
she hugs and smothers us,
tries to mother us . . .

The Alien

The alien
Was as round as the moon.
Five legs he had
And his ears played a tune.
His hair was pink
And his knees were green,
He was the funniest thing I'd seen
As he danced in the door
Of his strange spacecraft,
He looked at me —
And laughed and laughed!

Julie Holder

12

But we never know when
she'll turn grumposaurus,
we never know when,
mouth-wide, she'll roar at us,
or sit in a huff
and just ignore us.
It's a tough life
living with a grumposaurus.

Brian Moses

Mistaken Identity

I thought I'd seen a monster
From Outer Outer Space,
Till Dad said, 'No, it's just your mum
With a mud-pack on her face . . .'

Clive Webster

Make Your Own Monster: A DIY Guide

How do you make a monster?

Not with the glare of a torch-eye
slicing into the dark;
not with a gash of yellow paint
or the swing of a bat-wing cloak.
Nor with the roar of a dinosaur
or a sudden ruler-crack,
nor with egg-boxes, staples, glue . . .

This is what you do . . .

You lie awake after twilight
under a starless sky;
you leave your window just ajar
and feel the night creep by.
When the window squeaks
you start to sweat,
you remember the wind is still
and yet . . .
A creak in the hall
crawls on to the stair
and you know that somehow,
something is there . . .

Your mouth is dry
and the hairs on your back
stand to attention,
stopped in their track.
And a shadow crouches
by the door . . .
gathers breath
then slowly creeps

across the floor

TOWARDS YOU!

Then, you can be sure,
you've made your monster!

Judith Nicholls

14

The Night of the Junk Monsters

'In the time I've been school caretaker
I've seen many a curious sight,
But nothing so strange, or mad or daft
As what I saw last night.
There were five junk monsters dancing —
The ones made by 4C —
Whooping it up in the school hall.
Scared the daylights out of me!'

'Tell me again, please. And slowly.'

'Well, I'd been down to the pub,
Saw these lights in school on my way home —
Too late for an after-school club.
I looked in through the big hall window
And I nearly had a fit:
That robot thing made of soap powder packs
Going mad on the school drum kit!
The other four laughing and lumbering round
In some sort of dance or chase,
That dangly one with the coat hangers
Seemed to be setting the pace.
And the nasty, blobby, green one,
It's made from some curtains, I think,
Was laughing and heaving and wobbling away
With the snaky one that's pink.
I must have been there at the window
Half an hour with both eyes popping;
I left them at it in the end —
They showed no sign of stopping.'

16

'Well, I've checked on your midnight monsters,
I've been down to that classroom just,
And they're all safely back in their places,
Lifeless and gathering dust.
It's a really fantastic story . . .'

'Headmaster, it happened that way!'

'Let's go through it just once more:
You'd been down to the pub, you say . . .'

Eric Finney

The Monster's Heart

My master made me, chose each part,
then set me living, with a heart,
a hopeful, human heart.

His monstrous skill encased within
an envelope of tortured skin,
the muscles, sinews, bones, the brain
that works my body, knows my pain.
I lurched, I lumbered in the light,
but each one turned from me in fright;
I looked for love, encountered dread,
and learned that I were better dead.
The human world is not a place
to welcome this inhuman face,
so now I hide in bitter shade,
and curse the day that I was made.

I curse my maker and his art,
but most of all, I curse my heart,
my lonely, human heart.

Rowena Sommerville

18

Epitaph for Frankenstein

When Frankenstein's Monster finally died,
And his reign of terror ceased,
These were the words they inscribed on his grave:
'May the occupant Rust in Peace.'

Clive Webster

Watch Your Teacher Carefully

It happened in school last week
when everything seemed fine
assembly, break, science, and spelling
three twelves are four times nine.

But then I noticed my teacher
scratching the skin from her cheek
a forked tongue flicked from her lips
her nose hooked into a beak.

Her twenty arms grew longer
they ended in terrible claws
by now she was orange and yellow and green
with crunching great teeth in her jaws.

Her twenty eyes were upon me
as I ran from the room for the Head
got to his office, burst through the door
met a bloodsucking alien instead.

Somehow I got to the staffroom
the doorknob was dripping with slime
inside were seven hideous things
who thought I was dinner time.

I made my escape through a window
just then a roaring sound
knocked me over flat on my face
as the whole school left the ground.

Powerful rockets pushed it
back into darkest space
all I have left are the nightmares
and these feathers that grow on my face.

David Harmer

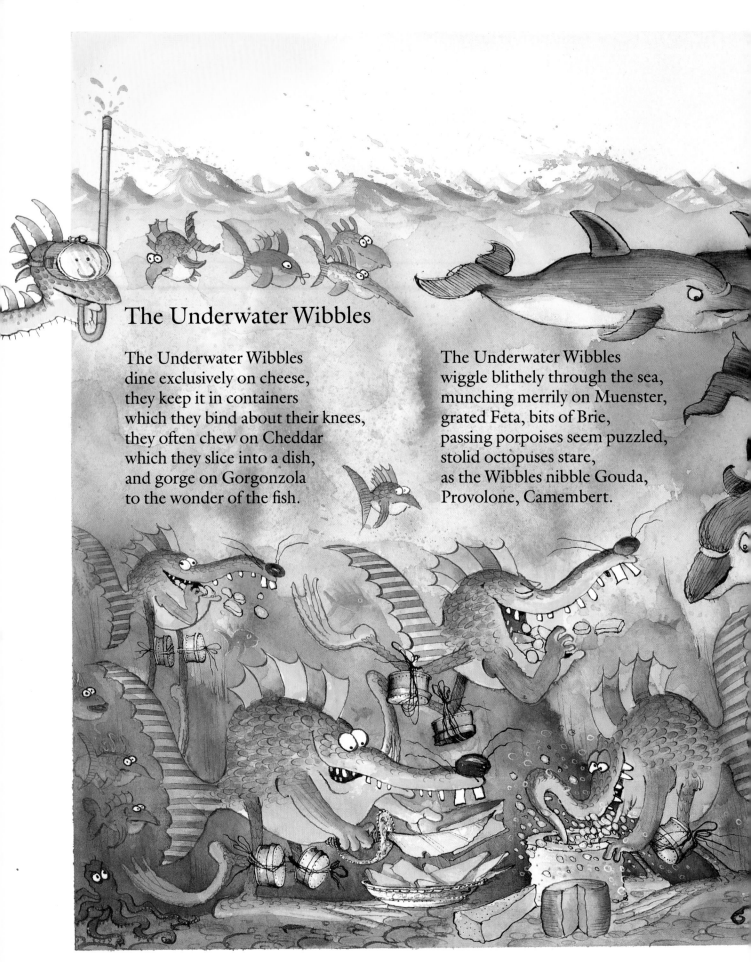

The Underwater Wibbles

The Underwater Wibbles
dine exclusively on cheese,
they keep it in containers
which they bind about their knees,
they often chew on Cheddar
which they slice into a dish,
and gorge on Gorgonzola
to the wonder of the fish.

The Underwater Wibbles
wiggle blithely through the sea,
munching merrily on Muenster,
grated Feta, bits of Brie,
passing porpoises seem puzzled,
stolid octopuses stare,
as the Wibbles nibble Gouda,
Provolone, Camembert.

The Underwater Wibbles
frolic gaily off the coast,
eating melted Mozzarella
served on soggy crusts of toast,
Wibbles gobble Appenzeller
as they execute their dives,
oh, the Underwater Wibbles
live extraordinary lives.

Jack Prelutsky

23

The Sliver-Slurk

Down beneath the frogspawn,
Down beneath the reeds,
Down beneath the river's shimmer,
Down beneath the weeds,
Down in dirty darkness,
Down in muddy murk,
Down amongst the sludgy shadows
Lives the Sliver-slurk;

Lives the Sliver-slurk
And the Sliver-slurk's a thing
With a gnawing kind of nibble
And a clammy kind of cling,
With a row of warts on top
And a row of warts beneath
And a horrid way of bubbling through
Its green and stumpy teeth;

With its green and stumpy teeth,
Oh, the Sliver-slurk's a beast
That you'd never find invited
To a party or a feast —
It would terrify the guests,
Make them shake and shout and scream,
Crying: 'Save us from this loathsomeness,
This monster from a dream!'

It's a monster from a dream,
Haunting waters grey and grim,
So be careful where you paddle
Or go happily to swim:
It is down there, it is waiting,
It's a nasty piece of work
And you might just put your foot upon
The slimy Sliver-slurk.

Richard Edwards

24

Be Wary of the Werewolf Wild

Be wary of the werewolf wild,
he's very big and hairy.
His favourite meal's a little child.
His favourite mode is scary.

His claws are black and sharp and long.
His eyes are gruesome red.
His teeth are yellow, sharp and strong.
He howls when we're in bed.

At dead of night he starts to creep,
and prowl in pale moonlight.
Is there a child not yet asleep?
He's feeling like a bite.

So go to bed and go to sleep
as soon as you are able
or you will be in trouble deep
in a dish on a werewolf's table.

Michaela Morgan

26

The Glamdrak

Over the hill the Glamdrak came,
its claws were large,
its eyes aflame.

Across the fields the Glamdrak strode,
straddled the fence,
and stood on the road.

Into the town the Glamdrak walked,
with poisoned breath
its quarry it stalked.

In the square the Glamdrak paused,
and screeched its fury
at all the locked doors.

Past the church the Glamdrak went,
into the distance,
its anger spent.

Robin Mellor

27

Three of a Kind

I stalk the timberland,
I wreck and splinter through,
I smash log cabins,
I wrestle grizzly bears.
At lunch-time if I'm dry
I drain a lake or two,
I send the wolves and wolverines
Howling to their lairs.
I'm Sasquatch,
Bigfoot,
Call me what you like,
But if you're a backpacker
On a forest hike,
Keep a watch behind you,
I'm there, though rarely seen.
I'm Bigfoot,
Sasquatch,
I'm mean, mean, mean.

I pad across the snow field,
Silent as a thief,
The phantom of the blizzard,
Vanishy, rare.
I haunt the barren glacier
And men in disbelief
Goggle at the footprints
I scatter here and there.
I'm Abominable,
Yeti,
Call me what you choose,
But if you're a mountaineer,
Careful when you snooze,
I'm the restless roaming spirit
Of the Himalayan Range.
I'm Yeti,
Abominable,
I'm strange, strange, strange.

I rear up from the waves,
I thresh, I wallow,
My seven snaky humps
Leave an eerie wake.
I crunch the silly salmon,
Twenty at one swallow,
I tease the silly snoopers —
A fiend? A fish? A fake?
I'm The Monster,
Nessie,
Call me what you please,
But if you're a camper
In the lochside trees,
Before you zip your tent at night
Say your prayers and kneel.
I'm Nessie,
The Monster,
I'm real, real, real.

Richard Edwards

The Truth about the Abominable Footprint

The Yeti's a Beast
Who lives in the East
    And suffers a lot from B.O.
His hot hairy feet
Stink out the street
    So he cools them off in the snow.

Michael Baldwin

29

The Snow Monster

When the Snow Monster sneezes,
Flurries of snow swirl and whirl,
Twisting round trees, curling into crevices,
Brushing the ground a brilliant white.

When the Snow Monster bellows,
Blizzards blot out the sky,
Piling up drifts, blocking roads,
Burying the landscape in a white grave.

When the Snow Monster cries,
Soft flakes slip and slide gently down
Into the hands of waiting children
Who test their taste with their tongues.

When the Snow Monster sleeps,
The air crackles with children's laughter
As they throw snowballs, build snowmen
And whizz downhill on their sledges.

John Foster

The Fire Monster

Deep in the boiling belly
Of the volcano
The Fire Monster sleeps:
Wisps of smoke from his nostrils
Squeeze through cracks
In the crater's mouth.

Deep in the boiling belly
Of the volcano
The Fire Monster stirs:
Bubbles of lava from his lips
Foam through crevices
And simmer beneath the surface.

Deep in the boiling belly
Of the volcano
The Fire Monster wakes:
Jets of lava gush from his throat,
Squirting through fissures,
Bursting the crater's dam.

Deep in the boiling belly
Of the volcano
The Fire Monster roars:
Huge chunks of rock spit from his mouth.
Red torrents of lava shoot into the sky,
Then stream down the crater's sides.

In the village in the valley,
The watchers wait
For the Fire Monster's anger to abate.

John Foster

The Last Monster

We are the people marching together
With drums loud as thunder and swords at our sides,
Through forests and deserts and cruel grey weather
To the cave in the rocks where the last monster hides.
We are the people marching together
To challenge the terrible beast in its den,
To catch it, to drag it back home on a tether
So children need never fear monsters again.
We are the people marching.

I am the last monster, waiting and weary,
Shivering all day in the chill from the ground,
Life's not worth living now, everything's dreary,
Cramped in this cave as the fog swirls around.
I am the last monster, waiting and weary,
Once I was furious, fearsome and bold,
Once my eyes glittered, but now they're all bleary,
Nothing's so sad as a monster grown old.
I am the last monster, waiting.

Richard Edwards